BIBLE INSIGHTS: BIBLE BOOK STUDIES FOR YOUTH

ROMANS

All Right!

By Tom Couser

CPH
SAINT LOUIS

Edited by Thomas A. Nummela

Rachel C. Hoyer, editorial associate

We solicit your comments and suggestions concerning this material. Please write to Product Manager, Youth Bible Studies, CPH, 3558 S. Jefferson Avenue, St. Louis, MO 63118-3968.

Scripture taken from the HOLY BIBLE, NEW INTERNATIONAL VERSION®. NIV® Copyright © 1973, 1978, 1984 by International Bible Society. Used by permission of Zondervan Publishing House. All rights reserved.

Copyright © 1996 Concordia Publishing House
3558 S. Jefferson Avenue, St. Louis, MO 63118-3968
Manufactured in the United States of America

1   2   3   4   5   6   7   8   9   10   05   04   03   02   01   00   99   98   97   96

Contents

Welcome to *Bible Insights!*

Welcome to the *Bible Insights* series of Bible studies for youth! These materials are designed to provide study opportunities that explore selected books of the Bible in depth and apply the wisdom these books impart to the real-life issues young people face. Each book in this series has been carefully prepared to speak to the needs and concerns of youth, providing insight from God's Word. Each book consists of four sessions of study and can be used for weekly group Bible study, individual study, or a Bible-study retreat or seminar.

This book is designed for the leader of the sessions. It provides all the information and instructions necessary for an effective Bible study. Each study includes material you can reproduce for the students in your group. Additional information on the Bible book to be studied and some helpful information about small-group Bible studies are included in the Introduction.

May God bless your study by the Spirit's power, as you lead young people to greater insight about God's Word and the good things God desires to bring through it to their lives.

Introduction
to the Book of Romans

Purpose and Theme

Young people live in a world of high expectations. The pressure to measure up to the world's standards is strong. The result can be a feeling of inferiority and brokenness. Young people may question their worth and value—in their own eyes, and in the eyes of their family, their friends, and their God.

The apostle Paul was like that. As a New Testament convert to Christianity, Paul experienced firsthand the Gospel of Jesus Christ. He was well aware of his shortcomings, his sinfulness. He knew the contrast between life with Christ and life without Him. And he knew the love of God that transformed his life and led him to a new awareness of God's unique view of those for whom Christ died. For Christ's sake, God does not see our sinfulness and shame—He sees the new life worked in us by the Holy Spirit.

That same Good News can touch the lives of young people today. The Gospel's power can set them free from the bondage of human expectations and sin. It assures each child of God that they are loved, restored, and made new through Jesus Christ. They are *all right*.

Author and Setting

The epistle to the Romans was written by the familiar apostle Paul, one known as Saul from Tarsus, but made new in heart and mind by Christ Himself on the Damascus road. Paul stands out in New Testament history as one of the greatest missionaries for Jesus Christ in any age. His first three missionary journeys took him through much of Asia Minor and Greece. Everywhere Paul went he planted churches. Paul excelled at training leaders and then empowering them to continue the work of sharing the Gospel in that place, while Paul himself moved on.

Paul kept in touch with these mission stations, and those who served them, through letters (most Bibles call them *epistles*, a word rooted in the Greek language in which those letters were written). Many of Paul's letters are found in our Bibles, including nine to various congregations or groups of churches and four more personal letters to individuals. One of those letters will be the focus of this study, the epistle to the Christians in Rome.

The Church in Rome

At the time this epistle was written, Paul had yet to visit Rome. However, he still felt a close affiliation with the Roman Christians.

As it conquered and occupied new territory, the Roman government displaced many people. Those with special skills were often moved to where they were needed. As the capital of the empire, Rome served as the government's center. The most gifted and skilled were summoned there to work for the Emperor himself. **Rome, however, was not a great place to live for everyone. Historians estimate that 40 percent of its residents were slaves. Another 30 percent of its residents faced poverty through unemployment, displaced from jobs by slaves. Only 5 percent may have experienced significant wealth and privilege.**

The Christian living in Rome came from **many** places. They probably had an elitist attitude. They were, after all, (1) living in Rome, (2) people of means, and (3) enlightened with this new knowledge of Jesus Christ. They had reason to be proud. **Scholars generally agree that while the church in Rome was comprised predominantly of Gentiles, a substantial minority were likely converted Jews. These proud "descendants of Abraham" may have been even more arrogant than other Romans.**

Paul had much in common with these Christians in Rome. Like many of them, he was a Jew; in fact he had been a Pharisee. While he did not live in Rome, he was a Roman citizen. He also had been enlightened by the Good News. As such, Paul could not only identify with the Roman Christians, he could also understand their struggles. He knew the difficulties they would face in hearing and proclaiming the Gospel message. Paul uses this letter to point out to the Christians in Rome—and to us—that salvation is not merited or earned. It matters not who we are because, "All have sinned and fall short of the glory of God" **(Romans 3:23).** Paul's epistle to the Romans is perhaps the clearest presentation of the Good News apart from the gospels themselves.

A Few Suggestions for Your Study

1. Use a variety of learning styles. Remember, everyone learns differently. Most teens learn best through experience. With that in mind, various activities are used to introduce the lesson themes.

2. The lesson plans offer some options. Each lesson contains more material than you will need. This gives you the opportunity to select activities that fit your group. Be sensitive to the needs of the young people in your class. Listen to them and respond to their needs.

3. Active learning fits the needs of contemporary youth. Young people live in a fast-paced world. Limit any activity to 15 minutes. Allow discussions to flow freely. Encourage participants to express their feelings as well as their thoughts.

4. Relax and have fun. If the young people see you putting yourself into the lesson, they will follow along. Be yourself. Talk about your faith struggles. By sharing your feelings you will give students permission to share theirs.

5. Invite the young people to bring their own Bibles and to record insights about the text.

6. Occasionally, you may want everyone to use the same version of the Bible. This will help the group focus on the lesson without becoming lost in the different translations and interpretations.

7. Several times students will be asked to read aloud a section of Scripture. In those situations, ask for volunteers. However, if you must select someone, choose a capable and confident student. Never use reading the Bible as a punishment for misbehavior in class.

8. After a Bible reading, check to make sure all the students understand important words and phrases. Taking time to clarify concepts will make your class more meaningful for your students.

9. When you ask the class to complete an exercise within a given time, be sure to give a two- and then a one-minute warning before you call the class back to order.

10. If your group is larger than eight, consider working in two or more groups when the lesson calls for discussion or personal sharing.

11. Model the behaviors, the confidentiality, and the vulnerability you expect from your class. You have the position and opportunity to increase the spiritual depth of your discussion by your actions. Protect the person who risks sharing from the heart, and encourage your students to give their full attention to the words of their peers.

Building Relationships

Jesus desires to be our close friend as we take our daily walk of discipleship. It is beneficial to have Christian friends who can support us in that journey. Hopefully, this class will enable some of those relationships to develop. It begins with you.

Take time to get to know the members of your class. The most important time in any session is the 10–15 minutes before class begins. You need to be prepared to teach prior to that time. Be ready to greet the students as they arrive. Listen with interest as they talk about the things going on in their lives.

Try to spend some time outside of class with your students. Eating together is a great relationship-builder. Call them on the telephone just to talk. Remember their birthdays and recognize each special achievement with a card or note.

Strive to build relationships within the class as well. Encourage small-group discussions. Be sensitive to those who might be left on the outside. Attempt to help the others understand their situation in the hope that they will seek to include them. Do your best to promote class unity.

Teacher/Student Relationships

Our teaching may only be as strong as our relationships with our class members. As we learn to know our students—and as they learn to know us—our ability to direct our teaching to their lives and their ability to listen both improve.

Some suggestions:
- *Maintain a balance* between being the teacher and being a friend. You're not a teenager. And you don't need to be one or act like one to relate to your class. Your are, however, a potentially significant person in the lives of your students. Many young people seek adults with whom they can relate and on whom they can count.

- *Don't talk down to your students.* High school students see themselves as "no longer children." They will relate best to adults who give them credit for all their strengths and potential, and who are gentle with reminders that they have some areas in their lives in which they need to grow. Resist sarcasm, teasing, and put-downs of any kind.
- *Participate with your students* in class activities. Share your own responses as examples to the students. If you ask students to cut, paste, or draw, be a willing participant in the activity. It will quickly blunt any perception that such activities are childish.
- *Sit, if possible.* With a small group, in a single circle, or around a table, sit at the same level as your class. Stand when leading several small groups or in a situation where all the participants may not be able to see you otherwise.
- *Refrain from "teacher only" privileges.* If food or drink is not allowed for the students, finish yours before you enter the room or save it until after class. If refreshments are appropriate, make sure they are available to the entire class.

If your group is small, you may be able to participate in one of the small-group discussions during class. If more than two or three groups form, it may be wiser to "float" among the groups. Recognize that young people may filter their responses and opinions with an adult present in their small group.

Be sensitive to the feelings of your students. As you respect them, they will grow in their respect for you.

(From *Bible Impact, Book 4*, page 73, © 1994 CPH. All rights reserved.)

Teaching without Student Pages

In response to the requests of many teachers, the Bible Insights studies are designed with Student Pages that you may duplicate. However, your class may be getting tired of a steady diet of study sheets, or perhaps you or your students simply don't like them. You may wish to omit some and use others. Or you may wish to do without them entirely. Here are some suggestions for adapting the lessons:

- Write response activities (sentence completions, multiple-choice questions, or true/false statements) on the chalkboard or newsprint before class. Students can still respond and discuss in small groups or as a whole class.
- Write Bible references and discussion questions on index cards. Distribute the cards to individual students or small groups at the appropriate time.
- Adapt Student Page activities so they can be done without the sheet of paper. For example, rather than having the students mark a set of response scales on a Student Page, have them stand at imaginary points along the longest wall of your classroom. The wall becomes the scale as you read the response statements.
- You can frequently lead a class discussion from questions on the

Student Page or invite small groups to discuss the questions one at a time.

- For some activities, you can have the students respond on blank paper or draw their own version of the Student Page illustration before completing the activity.
- Omit activities that are strictly paper-oriented and substitute more active ones. Even teenagers enjoy simple games and *active* learning assignments.
- If no other solution is obvious, scan the Student Page activity to determine the purpose it serves in the progression of the lesson and summarize that point directly. Or invent another method of communicating it to the students.

Evaluation

Evaluation should be a part of every session. Take time after each session to reflect on activities that went well or didn't work and why, concepts some students didn't grasp, and new issues or concerns you heard from your students.

Occasionally, take time after class to discuss with at least a few of the students the following questions: What was the best part of the class session today? If you were the teacher, what things would you do differently? What is the most important thing that you learned?

Incorporate the things you learn into your future lesson planning.

Am I All Right?

(Romans 3:9–26)

Focus

Teenagers often admit feeling insecure and anxious because of the expectations placed on them by society—and by those they place on them themselves. The pressure to conform is strong. But the world's gauge for success is a sham. The perfect image portrayed in the media is a fraud. The reality is that all people are sinners. That sinful nature is a result of original sin. No one is perfect! God has responded to our sinful imperfection by sending His Son, Jesus Christ, into the world as our Lord and Savior.

Objectives

That by the power of the Holy Spirit the participants will
1. recognize the sinful nature of all humanity;
2. better appreciate the righteousness that comes from God through faith in Jesus Christ;
3. through daily personal examination of themselves, in light of the Law, recognize their sinful nature and celebrate the forgiveness of sins.

Materials Needed

- Bibles
- Pencils or pens
- Newsprint and markers
- Copies of Student Pages 1–4
- Two identical cups or dishes, one broken in pieces and one perfect, and glue
- Christian stickers (obtained at local Christian bookstore) or blank labels

Lesson Outline: Am I All Right?

Activity	Minutes	Materials Needed
Warmup	10	Copies of Student Page 1, map of the New Testament world, broken cup and glue
A Sin Is a Sin	10	Copies of Student Page 2, Bibles, pencils or pens
The Debt Is Paid	15	Copies of Student Page 3, Bibles, pencils or pens
*Just Right*eousness	10	Copies of Student Page 4, Bibles, pencils or pens, newsprint and markers
Wrap-up	15	Unbroken cup, stickers or blank labels

Preparation

Some "props" will be helpful in teaching the concepts in this lesson; you will need to gather them in advance. At the beginning and end of the lesson you will use a pair of identical, breakable cups or dishes. You may be able to find cheap ones at a local discount store or garage sale. You may not wish to borrow from your kitchen since one of them will be damaged beyond repair. It may be helpful to put a large piece of poster board under the broken dish when it is displayed so that the broken pieces can be picked up easily. Glue is optional.

An option to the cup/dish activity is found in "Extending This Lesson." It involves a small mirror and bar of soap.

You will also need stickers with affirming messages from your local Christian bookstore or blank labels, such as address labels, and markers. Have enough labels or stickers so that each student will have four or five.

Warmup

New Testament Christians in Rome

As the students enter, have copies of "New Testament Christians in Rome" (Student Page 1) available. Locate a large wall map of the New Testament world and display it for the students. If the map has Paul's missionary journeys highlighted, point them out to the students. Remind the students of Paul's ministry and of how he planted churches in the various cities he visited.

Distribute copies of "New Testament Christians in Rome" (Student Page 1). Refer to the box in the lower right, highlighting the living situation for those Christians. Expand on this brief summary with details from the introduction. Discuss the circumstances in Rome with questions such as these: "What problems might these Christians have faced?" (Isolation from friends and relatives, life in a foreign land, persecution from non-Christians, both Jews and Romans.) "What advantages might living in Rome offer?" (Living in a large, modern city such as Rome may have offered many conveniences: large, well-supplied markets; good roads for those who traveled to other places; access to government; and plentiful employment, if one were well connected. The city's poor would not have experienced these benefits, however.) "What reason did the Christians in Rome have for being proud?" (Many were Jews or Romans citizens, some were wealthy, some were workers with specific skills, they knew about Jesus Christ.) "What obstacles had to be overcome to present the Gospel to them?" (They might not have seen a need for a Savior. Acknowledging Jesus was an intellectual experience, rather than a spiritual experience.)

A Broken Cup

Prior to class, locate two identical inexpensive china cups, glasses, or dishes. Place one in a bag and drop it on a hard floor so that it breaks into pieces. Have the pieces, and glue if you wish, out on a table as the students enter the room. Keep the second cup out of sight in a box or bag.

Tell the students that you dropped the cup and it broke. Explain that you feel badly and now wonder if it's possible to glue the cup back together so that it can still be used. You may wish to allow them to try to reassemble the cup. As they work, discuss the following questions: "Is it possible to get the cup back together? Even if all the pieces fit together, will we be able to glue them that way? Can the cup ever be used for its intended purpose again? How is the broken cup like our sinful nature?" (Our lives are broken. We can never be perfect in this life.)

At this point remove the broken pieces to the box or bag without revealing the second cup and place it aside. You will return to it at the end of the lesson.

A Sin Is a Sin

Pass out copies of "A Sin Is a Sin" (Student Page 2). Lead the class in reading **Romans 3:10b** in unison. Inform the class that there is a difference between how the world views sin and how a Christian views it. Remind the students that people use various words to cover up or disguise what God tells us is wrong. Point out the various euphemisms for the word *sin* on the Student Page. Ask students to suggest additional words. (Examples: *failure, a little problem,* or *goof-up.* You can expand this concept to include things the world does not see as sin: alternative lifestyles, cohabitation, and abortion.)

Ask the students to read **Romans 3:10b–18** silently. Then ask that they record a written response to the two questions that follow on the Student Page. Allow no more than five minutes for them to finish the assignment.

After five minutes, or when you sense everyone has completed the assignment, call the group together. Ask volunteers to share their responses to the two questions. (Possible responses might be: [1] Sin is doing bad things, and [2] Everyone is guilty.)

Before moving on, direct the students to again look at **Romans 3:11–12.** Point out that Paul views sin as turning away from God. When we turn away from God on a daily basis we risk becoming "worthless"— unable to serve Him and do His will.

Continue the discussion with the following questions:

1. What is original sin? (Original sin is the sinful nature all children inherit from their parents.)

2. What is the result of turning away from God? (Paul describes various implications [**Romans 3:13–18**]. The end result is that we say and do things that hurt God and others. In time such actions will make us very unhappy. Ultimately they lead to death and eternal damnation.)

3. How do you feel when the Bible describes you as standing guilty before God? (We feel ashamed. We're disappointed in our actions.)

The Debt Is Paid

Distribute copies of "The Debt Is Paid" (Student Page 3). Give the students a few moments to read and reflect on the invoice for sin.

If there are five or more students in your class, divide them into smaller groups of three to five students. Ask each small group to read **Romans 3:21–22** and then discuss the printed questions. Allow about eight minutes for the groups to discuss the questions.

Review with the entire class their responses to the questions. (Note: Even if these concepts seem basic and common knowledge, review them. The concept of justification by grace, apart from the Law, is the cornerstone of the Christian faith. It is worth repeating.) Possible responses to the questions might be as follows:

1. **Romans 3:21a.** Righteousness comes from God.
2. **Romans 3:22a.** Jesus Christ makes it possible.
3. **Romans 3:22b.** Everyone who believes in Him as Savior receives it.
4. It makes me feel joyful.
5. We no longer feel guilty and are free to serve God.

Just Righteousness

Distribute copies of "*Just Right*eousness" (Student Page 4). Point out that the word *righteous* is probably not part of our normal vocabulary. It is a word, however, that God uses when He looks at us in light of Jesus Christ's death on the cross and resurrection victory.

Direct the participants back into their small groups. Using the three Scripture passages listed, they are to develop a definition for righteousness. As they work, distribute sheets of newsprint paper and markers. Ask each group to write out their definition.

After five minutes, call the group together. Ask each group to hold up their newsprint and share their responses. (Typical responses might be as follows: Righteousness means to be like Jesus or to appear holy before God.) Direct the students to look up **Isaiah 64:6** and **Romans 3:20**. Pose the next question, "How much value does our personal righteousness have?" (No value at all.) Direct the students to the final question, "How is our righteousness made possible?" **Romans 3:24** makes it clear. It comes through Jesus Christ.

Wrap-up

The Perfect Cup

Remind the students about the broken cup and retrieve the bag into which you placed it. Pull out the perfect cup. The students will catch on quickly that this is no trick at all, that the perfect cup was in the bag the whole time. Say, "You're right! The only miracle here is the way God has healed our brokenness. God's gift of Jesus Christ heals the brokenness of sin. Looking at the many broken pieces of the cup makes us realize there is no way to make it perfect again. Our sinful brokenness has even greater implication, eternal death. We are healed only through Jesus."

Affirmation Stickers

Before the session, purchase Christian stickers from your local Christian bookstore. Stickers with any affirmation messages (God Loves You,

You Are Special, etc.) would be appropriate. Distribute the stickers, giving each person four or five.

When everyone has their stickers, tell them that they are to share the message of salvation through grace with other members of the class. When instructed to begin, they are to place the stickers on other class members. As they do so they are to say, "You are righteous in God's eyes."

Keep some stickers for yourself. Take time to recognize class members who are being overlooked by the others. Place the stickers on them using the same words.

If you cannot locate Christian stickers you can use blank adhesive labels to make your own. (Standard address labels work well.) Give each student up to five labels and ask them to write the affirmation messages on their labels—God Made You Special, You're a Neat Person, You Are Loved by God, etc.

Encourage the students to wear their stickers as they leave the class. During the rest of the Sunday morning activities, it will give them the opportunity to share their experience in the class. As an alternative, you could ask participants to save one or two stickers and to share them with members of the congregation.

Closing Prayer

Gather the students in a circle and close with the following prayer: "Gracious Lord, You have made us righteous through the gift of Your Son. Through His efforts our sins are forgiven. Now we can look forward to eternal life. May that Good News motivate us to share His love this day and always. Amen."

Extending This Lesson

If you have extra time, or as a substitute for the cup activity, you could share this activity with the students. Hold a mirror up for the students to see. Ask, "What is a mirror good for?" (Mirrors help us see our face and other places not normally visible to us. They help us see what we look like to others.) Ask, "When do you regularly look at yourself in a mirror each day?" (Most will use a mirror every morning as they prepare for the day.)

Point out that God's Law is like a mirror. It shows us what we really look like without the benefits of faith in Jesus Christ—sinful human beings. Then draw an outline of a cross on the mirror with the edge of a bar of soap. Remind the students that God sees us through the cross—not as sinful people, but as people for whom Christ died, righteous and holy by His grace. Suggest that each morning is a good time to remember these two key pictures of ourselves—sinful and made righteous by Christ. One way to do this would be to draw a similar cross on the bathroom mirror they regularly use. It would be a reminder to celebrate the forgiveness we have in Christ.

New Testament Christians in Rome

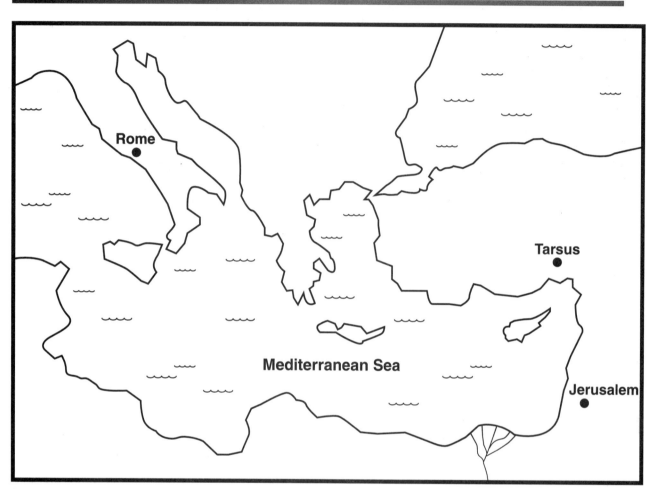

Rome

Tarsus

Mediterranean Sea

Jerusalem

Roman Christians

Jews and Gentile converts
Citizens of Rome
Skilled workers
Followers of Jesus Christ

Romans, Student Page 1

A Sin Is a Sin

"There is no one righteous, not even one" **(Romans 3:10b)**.

"Everyone does it"

Mistake

WHITE LIE!

Accident

"I'm only human"

Weakness

The world uses a variety of terms to mask the word *sin.* Read **Romans 3:10b–18.**

1. What is sin?

2. Who is guilty of sin?

Romans, Student Page 2

The Debt Is Paid

Invoice for Sin

	Guilty
Lying	Guilty
Slandering others	Guilty
Dirty thoughts	Guilty
Idolatry	Guilty
Craving material things	Guilty
Envying others	Guilty
Disobeying parents	Guilty
Not honoring God	Guilty

PAID BY CHRIST

_____
Punishment by death

TOTAL DUE

Read **Romans 3:21–22**
Questions for discussion:
1. Where does our righteousness come from?

2. Who makes it possible?

3. Who receives it?

4. How does having the gift of righteousness make you feel?

5. What effect will the gift of righteousness make in your life?

Just Righteousness

"That sure is a righteous shirt you are wearing."

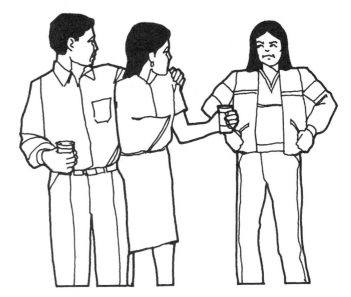

"You are really acting righteous tonight."

The word *righteous* is not usually part of our vocabulary. What does it really mean? Use the Scripture references below to develop your own definition of righteousness.

Philippians 1:10–11

1 Timothy 6:11

2 Peter 3:11

See the following passages to determine how much value our personal attempts at righteousness have.

Isaiah 64:6

Romans 3:20

How is our righteousness made possible?

Romans 3:22b–26

2 Corinthians 1:21–22

Romans, Student Page 4

Christ's Power
(Romans 3:27–5:11)

Focus

Young people live in a society that frequently honors and worships those who appear successful. Society seems to reward beauty, effort, and talent. God doesn't work that way. Our salvation is not effected or affected by our good deeds. Our salvation is a free gift. We are justified only by faith. That basic Christian truth needs to be applied to our lives, in our relationship with God and with others.

Objectives

That by the power of the Holy Spirit the participants will
1. understand justification by grace as the cornerstone of faith;
2. recognize the gift of justification by grace through faith as modeled by Abraham;
3. gain an appreciation for the fact that through Jesus Christ they have been reconciled with God;
4. see reconciliation at work in their own lives as they relate to others.

Materials Needed

- Bibles
- Pencils or pens
- Copies of Student Pages 5–8
- Marker board or newsprint and markers
- Video camera or tape player and blank tape (optional)

Lesson Outline: Christ's Power

Activity	Minutes	Materials Needed
Warmup	20	Copies of Student Page 5, video camera, tape and recorder (optional), marker board or newsprint and markers
Abraham's Story	15	Copies of Student Page 6, Bibles, pencils or pens, marker board or newsprint and markers
Reconciliation	15	Copies of Student Page 7, marker board or newsprint and markers
Paul's Formula	10	Copies of Student Page 8, Bibles, pencils or pens
Closing	5	

Preparation

The warmup activity, "Theological Nomenclature," suggests using video equipment to record several individuals giving the definitions of three theological terms: *justification, sanctification,* and *grace.* Video cameras are becoming more common. If you do not have one, perhaps one of your students' families or someone else in your church will have one. A tape recorder may be used instead.

If you plan ahead, you can assign a team of students to use a "man on the street" approach, randomly interviewing people on a street corner or in a shopping mall during the week prior to the lesson.

Another option would be to interview people from your church. This could be done during the week before class or on Sunday morning, before or after worship or before class. Ten to fifteen minutes of video tape should be sufficient. At the last minute, you could still catch one or two students on tape as they enter the room.

The most important 10 minutes in the session can be the time before the formal session. Try to spend time with each student. Ask how things are going in their lives. Be sincere as you ask about specific concerns or struggles they are facing.

Have copies of the Student Pages from the previous session available for those who were absent. Discuss the situation the Roman Christians faced. Review other key concepts in preparation for their participation in this session.

If you or your students have prepared a videotape, have a VCR and TV set up and ready to go.

Warmup

Opening Prayer

Open with a prayer like this one: "Gracious Lord, thank You for bringing us back together as Your children. Bless our time today as we discover the truths revealed in the Bible. Through the power of the Spirit, enable us to see how salvation has been won for us through the sacrifice of Jesus Christ. That's Good News for us and all people, since we have all fallen short of Your glory. Amen."

Theological Nomenclature

If you or your students produced a tape of interviews, introduce it by telling students that they are going to see individuals trying to define some religious terms. They will be discussing the same terms in class. As they listen, they are to consider which of the speakers has a good understanding of the terms and how their own definitions differ from those on the tape.

Write the following Scripture references on the board or on a sheet of newsprint.

Justification: **Romans 3:22–24, Romans 4:25**
Sanctification: **1 Corinthians 6:11, Titus 3:5**
Grace: **Ephesians 2:8–9**

If you have six or more students in your class divide the students into three small groups. Assign each group one of the words. If you have five or fewer students, allow them to work independently. Ask them to select one of the three words. (Check to make sure at least one person has taken each of the words.) Distribute copies of "Theological Nomenclature" (Student Page 5). Using the Scripture references, complete the sentences and provide a definition.

After five minutes call the group together and review responses. Suggested responses:

Justification. To be made perfect again in God's eye, "Just-as-if-I'd never sinned."

Sanctification. To be made holy by the blood of Jesus Christ.

Grace. The free gift of salvation.

Group Definitions

If you decide not to use the videotape, use the following activity as an alternative. If you have more than five students divide the class into small groups. Groups with three to five participants work best. Distribute copies of "Theological Nomenclature" (Student Page 5). Ask them to begin by writing definitions on their own. After 5 minutes encourage them to share their definitions with their group. When all have shared, have them combine all their thoughts into a group definition for each word. Give the students about 10 minutes to complete the above tasks.

Call the class together and write out the Scripture references listed above either on the board or on newsprint. Direct the students to their Bibles. Using the references, have them make changes or adjustments to their definitions. After about 5 minutes call the group together and discuss the changes they have made. Share the definitions printed above.

Abraham's Story

Distribute copies of "Abraham's Story" (Student Page 6). Introduce the activity by telling the students that Abraham was the patriarch of all Jews, including those living in Rome. Paul is attempting to convince them that Abraham was saved by God's grace, and not his good deeds. That concept was crucial for their faith, just as it is for ours.

There are six references identified on the map. Ask for volunteers to read them when the time comes. Before you begin, post the following questions on the board or on a sheet of newsprint.

1. What does Abraham do to deserve God's love?
2. What is it that saves Abraham? (Hint: see **Genesis 15:5–6.**)
3. What signs of the covenant does God give Abraham?
4. How does Abraham respond to God's covenant?

Using the Student Page as a reference, have the participants tell Abraham's story. At the conclusion discuss their responses to the questions you have posed. If you have used small groups previously, consider using them again to facilitate discussion.

Suggested responses:

1. Abraham did nothing to deserve God's love.

2. Abraham was saved by his faith, "He believed the Lord" (**Genesis 15:6, Romans 4:3, 18**).

3. Circumcision was the most obvious sign, but he also had the stars in the heavens.

4. Abraham responded by building altars and worshiping God.

Reconciliation

Print out this definition on the board or newsprint: "Reconciliation: To restore to friendship or harmony." Move the students into a discussion of the concept of reconciliation. Remind them that since the sin of Adam and Eve the relationship between God and man has been broken. God's covenant with Abraham was the initiation of the reconciliation process. That process was completed in Jesus Christ. God now wants us to be reconciled with each other. Tell the class that you are going to share a story of reconciliation.

Distribute copies of "A Story of Reconciliation" (Student Page 7). You may either read the story yourself or ask one of the students to share the story.

At the conclusion discuss the following questions with the class. If you have been using small groups to facilitate discussion, do so again.

1. What motivated Emma to hire the boys? (Her Christian concern for them and their future, and her own need for help.)

2. Why would it be hard for others, especially her sons, to understand her decision? (It would more "natural" for her to hate the boys and seek revenge against them.)

3. In the opinion of most people, would her decision be wise? (In the eyes of the world, Emma's decision was not a wise one. She could be endangering her own life.)

4. Why were Jesus' words in **Luke 23:34** so meaningful to Emma? (She may have understood that the boys were acting on impulse more than targeting her husband for violence, or that they did not fully understand the consequences of their actions. Jesus could forgive those who acted deliberately against Him, including you and me. His love for Emma empowered her to show love to others.)

5. What role does Jesus play in the reconciliation process? (Christ living in Emma motivated her actions. "We love because He first loved us" [1 John 4:19].)

6. What role does Emma play? (Emma reflected Christ's love to the boys.)

7. What role do the members of this Bible class play? (We can learn from Emma and her relationship with Christ. Christ loved and died for us.)

Paul's Formula

Distribute copies of "Paul's Formula" (Student Page 8). Inform the students that a Christian lifestyle of reconciliation involves a certain combination of things. Paul outlines this formula in **Romans 5:3–5.** Paul worked to apply the concept of reconciliation to his relationships. Ask students to think of obstacles that would have kept Paul from being forgiving toward others. (Hint: the picture at the top of the page portrays many of Paul's struggles.)

Using **Romans 5:3–5** as a guide, ask them to work individually at completing the Student Page. Inform the students that since the responses are personal they will not be asked to share what they have written. After five minutes call the class together and share the following typical responses with the students.

Suffering. We feel suffering when we are persecuted or made fun of because of our faith.

Perseverance. We persevere when we continue to worship God in spite of the persecutions we face.

Character. We have character when over time we, through the power of the Spirit, establish the lifestyle of a servant.

Hope. We have hope when we trust in Jesus Christ as our Savior.

Closing

Close the session with the following prayer: "Jesus, through Your suffering and death, You restored the relationship between us and Your Father. Now, through the power of the Spirit, make us reconcilers. Give us forgiving hearts and help us to daily share that forgiveness with others. Amen."

Theological Nomenclature

We often find ourselves facing words that are difficult to pronounce and understand. Some words that have become familiar and even part of our vocabulary have definitions that in reality may be unclear to us. It is important, however, that we know the correct meanings of these words since they relate to our faith and relationship with Jesus Christ.

Three such words are found below. Complete each of the sentences by explaining what you think each word means.

Justification is ...

Sanctification is ...

Grace is ...

Abraham's Story

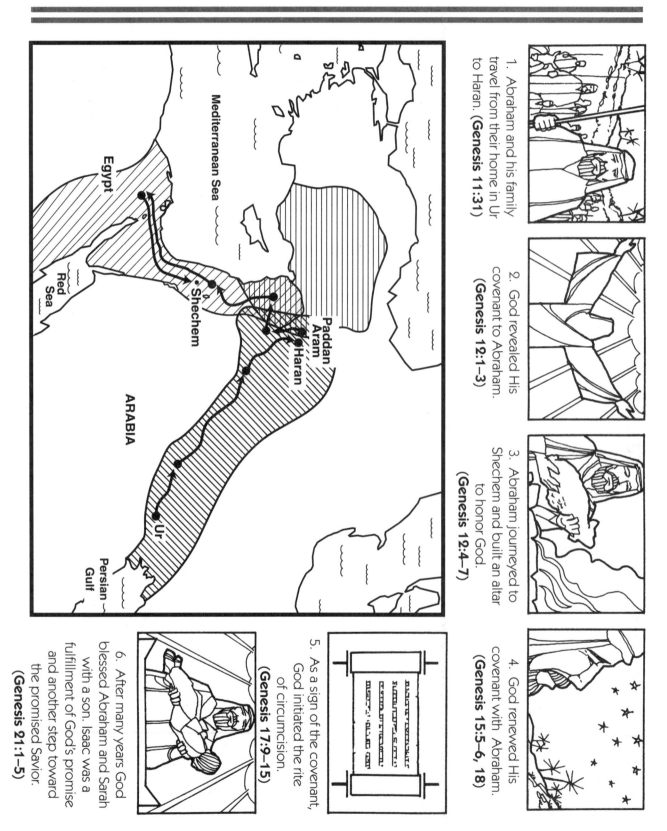

Mediterranean Sea

Egypt

Red Sea

Shechem

Paddan Aram

Haran

ARABIA

Ur

Persian Gulf

1. Abraham and his family travel from their home in Ur to Haran. **(Genesis 11:31)**

2. God revealed His covenant to Abraham. **(Genesis 12:1–3)**

3. Abraham journeyed to Shechem and built an altar to honor God. **(Genesis 12:4–7)**

4. God renewed His covenant with Abraham. **(Genesis 15:5–6, 18)**

5. As a sign of the covenant, God initiated the rite of circumcision. **(Genesis 17:9–15)**

6. After many years God blessed Abraham and Sarah with a son. Isaac was a fulfillment of God's promise and another step toward the promised Savior. **(Genesis 21:1–5)**

Romans, Student Page 6

A Story of Reconciliation

In many ways Emma could still not believe what she was doing. Still, she had made the decision and was confident things would work out.

Emma and her husband, Herman, had operated a small grocery store in the city for many years. However, over time, the quiet neighborhood had changed. The flower beds and backyard vegetable gardens were replaced by graffiti. More important, for Emma and Herman, the familiar faces of their mostly German neighbors disappeared. Taking their place were people from other races and cultures.

Emma and Herman talked of moving. They could sell the store and the apartment above it. With the money they could buy a home in the suburbs close to their sons. In the end they stayed. "This is our life," Herman declared. "Besides, people will always need bread and milk."

Emma and Herman attempted to get along with everyone. They even tried to help those who were less fortunate. They often let people buy food on credit, allowing them to pay when their checks arrived. With the exception of a few minor incidents of vandalism, the store continued to operate as it always had.

Then one day it happened. Herman had gone out into the alley to throw out the trash. Three boys jumped him. They wanted money, but Herman never carried a wallet. In frustration one of them hit him over the head. The blow left him lying in the dirt.

The boys didn't know they had left him dead. The shock of the mugging was too much for Herman's heart. He suffered a massive heart attack and died before anyone could help him.

Emma was heartbroken. The store was all she had. Herman was not just her husband, he was her partner. She closed the store for a few days, but the morning after the funeral, she opened for business again. Later that day a policeman stopped by. Herman's attackers had been arrested. They were kids from the neighborhood, at loose ends while their parents worked. As juveniles, and since Herman had died of a heart attack and not the beating, they might be released, but only with supervision. "I am worried about their future," the officer continued. "They seem repentant and say that it won't happen again. But without careful supervision, they could easily get in trouble again."

"I am going to need help with the store," Emma replied. "Maybe they could work for me. I will keep an eye on them."

Emma could hardly believe her own words! Herman was dead, and the boys were responsible. Now she was offering to help them. She would never be able to explain her decision to other people, especially her sons.

Later that night she said her prayers and pondered her decision. She knew in her heart that it was the right one. It was what Herman would have wanted her to do, she reflected. More than that, she knew it was what Jesus wanted her to do.

Emma fell asleep with her Bible open. One passage was underlined: "Father, forgive them, for they do not know what they are doing." **(Luke 23:34)**

© 1996 CPH   Scripture quotation: NIV®   **Romans, Student Page 7**

Paul's Formula

In **Romans 5:3–5** Paul reveals the formula for his success.

Suffering +	Perseverance +	Character =	Hope
I suffer when I …	I persevere when I …	I show character when I …	I have hope when I …

"And hope does not disappoint us, because …" (Romans 5:5)

   Scripture quotation: NIV®

Who's in Control?

(Romans 8)

Focus

Many young people long for the good life portrayed in the media. They tend to associate success with material things, financial security, and popularity. Yet by God's grace we know that the good life can only be found in Jesus Christ. Through Him we are "more than conquerors." In all things God, through the power of the Spirit, is in control.

Objectives

That by the power of the Holy Spirit the participants will

1. recognize the hardships in this world that sometimes come with being a disciple of Jesus Christ;
2. rejoice through the power of the Spirit that God promises to continue to overcome the barriers that could separate them from Christ;
3. live in joyful anticipation as they daily celebrate God's presence and the hope of future glory.

Materials Needed

- Bibles
- Pencils or pens
- Marker board or newsprint and markers
- Copies of Student Pages 9–11
- Alarm clock
- A large box
- Snacks and beverage (for anticipation party)
- Coin (optional)

Lesson Outline: Who's in Control?

Activity	Minutes	Materials Needed
Warmup	5	Large box and alarm clock, coin (optional)
Who's in Control?	10	Copies of Student Page 9
Barriers	10	Copies of Student Page 10
Confidence Posters	15	Copies of Student Page 11, newsprint and markers
Anticipation Party	15	Snacks and beverages

Preparation

In **Romans 8:18–25** Paul speaks of how "our present sufferings are not worth comparing with the glory that will be revealed in us." Paul lived his life in anticipation of that glory.

A major component of this lesson is an anticipation party which will give the students a sense of expectation and joyful celebration. You will want to spend some time planning and preparing for the party. Prepare or purchase the snacks to be served. The snacks could be cookies or donuts and a beverage (orange juice, soda, etc.). Simple decorations, streamers, party hats, etc., could add to the atmosphere. They are optional.

Add extra weight to a large box by placing heavy items (rocks or heavy books) in the bottom. Place prepared snacks in the box on top of the extra weight. You will want to seal the box with tape to conceal the contents. The box is going to serve as a heavy load during the warmup activity.

You will also need an alarm clock. Before the session, set the alarm to go off near the end of the class period. Make sure that the clock is in a conspicuous place in the classroom. Once the alarm goes off, the anticipation party is to begin; so set it to ring 45 or 50 minutes into the session, if your class lasts an hour. (If your class session is less than an hour, adjust the time accordingly.)

Warmup
Who Will Carry the Load?

Greet the students as they arrive. Hand one of the first students to enter the large box that you have prepared. Direct another student to find **Romans 8:18–21.** Ask them to be ready to read that portion of Scripture. It's important that the student who is carrying the box not put it down or be allowed to sit down until you instruct him or her to do so.

As additional students enter, tell the class that being a disciple for Jesus Christ can result in hardships. Continue by saying, "We can endure the earthly struggles because Jesus carried our load of sin and suffering for us on the cross, and we can live in joyful anticipation of eternal life in heaven." Ask the volunteer to read **Romans 8:18–21.** Tell the class that they are to be waiting in joyful anticipation during this session. Point out the alarm clock and tell them that when the alarm goes off, an anticipation party will begin. The box contains the snacks for the party. When you are ready to begin class, tell the person holding the box that he or she can put it down.

Or ...

The Hidden Coin

Play the following game. The only item you will need is a coin.

Show the students the coin. Tell them that you are going to put your hands behind your back. When you bring them out, the coin will be in one of the two hands. They must guess which hand it is in. Have the participants take turns. They get one point for each correct answer. The first person with three points wins. Have a small prize (candy, etc.) for the winner.

When the game is finished, point out that this was a game of anticipation. They were trying to anticipate which hand the coin was in. Guessing required taking a chance. As Christians we can anticipate eternal life, which does not involve a risk. Through Jesus' life, death, and resurrection, we are forgiven for our many sins. God promises that if we believe in Jesus Christ, we will have eternal life.

(As you conclude this activity, you may wish to use the alarm clock and snacks as suggested in "Who Will Carry the Load?" and have an anticipation party.)

Who's in Control?

Distribute copies of "Who's In Control?" (Student Page 9). The sheet contains the story of a boy who makes a tough decision. Ask for a volunteer to read the story aloud.

After the story has been read, divide the class into small groups to discuss "Some Things to Think About." If you have six or more students, divide the group into groups of three to five students.

After five minutes, briefly review the questions. Typical responses might be as follows:

1. It would have been easy for Tad to stay at the party. He also might have had a great time and not been tempted to consume alcohol.

2. Staying at the party meant he continued to face temptation to drink alcohol. He also might have found himself taking advantage of Tammy's inebriated state. Yes, he could have withstood sin's appeal but the risks were high.

3. The Spirit of God was in charge of Tad's life. Only through that power can we consistently resist temptation.

This discussion might give you the opportunity to talk about abstinence from alcohol before one is of legal age or sexual intercourse before marriage. Such decisions are not only God-pleasing but wise. They are also a strong Christian witness. Even as you share this message, reassure the participants that God does forgive those who have sinned.

Extending the Lesson

Paul alludes to his suffering in **Romans 8.** In **2 Corinthians 11:16–33** he gives a detailed account of his tribulations. Share Paul's account. Here is one way to do that: Make a tape recording of a person playing the role of St. Paul. On the tape, Paul would share all of his trials. The individual playing the role should end the account by saying, "When I reflect on my life, there is little doubt that God was in control."

Overcoming the Barriers

Point out that there are many barriers that could separate us from Christ and the path of discipleship He desires for us were it not for the fact that God overcomes those barriers by coming to us in Christ. Distribute copies of "Overcoming the Barriers" (Student Page 10).

If you used small groups for the previous activity, use them again now. Ask students to use the Scripture references to identify the barriers. Specific barriers should be written on the blank lines provided. Allow 10 minutes for the assignment.

After 10 minutes, or when you sense that everyone has finished, call the class together. Invite volunteers to share their answers. Typical responses might be as follows:

Romans 8:35: trouble, hardship, persecution, physical harm.

Romans 8:38–39: life or death, angels or demons, present power, future powers.

The message is clear. There is nothing that can separate us from the love and forgiveness won for us by Jesus Christ.

Words of Confidence

Distribute copies of "Words of Confidence" (Student Page 11).

Also provide each small group with a large sheet of newsprint and markers. Re-form the students in small groups or ask the class members to work with a partner at this time.

Tell the students that Paul's experiences—good and bad—served to strengthen his confidence. Paul was sure that God would not only protect him from all harm, but also give him the power he needed to follow God's will. **Romans 8** contains many statements that reinforce Paul's confidence in God's power. Many of those statements are printed on Student Page 11. Using those as examples, have the students develop contemporary slogans that will serve as reminders of God's promise. Share these sample slogans to get the students started: "Jesus Is Here! So You Can't Hurt Me!" or "Hang Out with Jesus and You're Gonna Hang Tough."

As the participants complete the assignment, post the slogans around the room. Allow the class members to continue with this task until the alarm goes off.

Anticipation Party

When the alarm goes off, call the class together. Allow the individual who initially carried the box at the beginning of the lesson to open it. Once the box is opened, allow the students to eat the snacks. If you have prepared a beverage, offer that at this time as well.

As the students eat the snacks, discuss the session, using the following questions:

1. "How did it feel having an alarm clock set to go off during class? Did you find the clock a distraction? What kinds of things kept you busy so you didn't think about the clock?"

2. "Did you anticipate the party? According to Paul, what kind of celebration was he anticipating?" **(Romans 8:19)** "How did anticipation of the celebration motivate him in his ministry?" **(8:24–25)**

3. "What keeps us from living each day of our lives in joyful anticipation of that celebration? How do we overcome those hurdles?"

Play an appropriate song during the party, such as "If God is for Us" by Degarmo and Key or "God Is in Control" by Twila Paris. You could also sing contemporary Christian songs such as: "We Shall Not Be Moved," "Rejoice in the Lord Always," or "We Shall Overcome." (These songs can be found in the songbook, *All God's People Sing* from Concordia Publishing House.)

As you close, reassure the participants by having one of the students read **Romans 8:37.** Remind them that Jesus Christ is the ultimate Conqueror. He conquered sin and death. In Him we too can be conquerors, both here on earth and in eternity.

Close the session with a prayer similar to this one: "Jesus, thank You for the assurance found in Your Word. Through the power of the Spirit, keep us mindful that You are the reason we can be so joyful. You are the reason we can celebrate! May that joy be part of our lives so that others may see our faith and be drawn to You. Amen."

Who's in Control?

Tad had come to the party with his friends, but it didn't take long for him to feel out of place. His good friend Chris had just been moved up to the varsity. It was the first time any of them had been invited to a "real" party. The beer was flowing freely and, with no adult in sight, things were getting wild.

Tammy, with a drink in her hand, wandered over to where he was standing. "Hi Tad," she cooed. "I'm surprised to see you here. I just know you're going to have a great time." Tad had always admired Tammy. He was surprised she even knew his name. This was his opportunity to make a move.

Instead, he found an excuse to slip away. He wasn't sure what motivated him, but he found himself in a convenience store down the street. He found a crumpled up business card in his wallet. Removing it, he punched in the numbers. A friendly voice on the other end answered.

"Dan, this is Tad. You always told me to call if I got in a situation where I didn't feel safe. Well, here I am."

Dan, the youth director from Tad's church, was there in 15 minutes. Dan offered to drive Tad home but asked if he wanted to talk first.

"No, I'll be alright," Tad answered. "I just can't figure it out. I still don't know what made me leave. My friends were there. We were going to have a great time. I know I'm going to take some teasing on Monday for walking out."

Dan listened intently, then he responded. "Tad, I think I know who was in charge of your life tonight."

Some Things to Think About

1. The situation Tad faced is familiar. Why would it have been easy for him to stay at the party? Would it have been wrong for Tad to stay at the party?

2. What temptations would Tad have faced if he stayed? Could Tad have stayed and not compromised his values?

3. Tad's youth counselor said, "I know who was in charge of your life tonight." What do you think he meant by that? If it was Tad's decision to leave the party, how could someone else be in charge? Who could that someone be? **(See Romans 8:9–11.)**

Overcoming the Barriers

Romans 8:35 _____
_____
_____
_____
_____

Romans 8:38 _____
_____
_____
_____
_____

Romans, Student Page 10

Words of Confidence

"In all things God works for the good of those who love Him."
(Romans 8:28)

"If God is for us, who can be against us?"
(Romans 8:31)

"Who will bring any charge against those whom God has chosen?"
(Romans 8:33)

"Who shall separate us from the love of Christ?"
(Romans 8:35a)

Scripture quotations: NIV®   © 1996 CPH

Therefore ... **4**
(Romans 12–13)

Focus

Young people live in a self-serving society. Even Christian young people may find the concept of sacrificial living foreign. But Christ calls His disciples to live for others. Christ is the ultimate example of sacrifice in His suffering and death. Through that sacrificial act He won salvation for all people and, by the power of the Holy Spirit, He moves us to reflect His love.

Objectives

That by the power of the Holy Spirit the participants will
1. contrast the self-centered life preferred by our sinful nature with the example of sacrificial life modeled by Jesus;
2. recognize that the power to be a servant/disciple comes only through God's Spirit;
3. rejoice in God's gift of His Spirit and be moved to a life of discipleship.

Materials Needed

- Bibles
- Pencils or pens
- Copies of Student Pages 12–16
- Pictures of contemporary servant heroes or of people serving
- Songbooks (optional for closing worship)

Lesson Outline: Therefore ...

Activity	Minutes	Materials Needed
Warmup	5–10	Pictures of people serving others
Heart of a Servant	5	Copies of Student Page 12
Be Transformed	10	Copies of Student Page 13, pencils or pens, and Bibles
Spiritual Gifts	15	Copies of Student Page 14, pencils or pens, and Bibles
My Mission Statement	10	Copies of Student Page 15, pencils or pens
Closing	5–10	Copies of Student Page 16, songbooks (optional)

Preparation

Search magazines and newspapers for pictures of people serving others. Typical photos could depict people building homes or serving in a hospital. If the youth group from your church has been involved in servant events or work camps, pictures from those activities would be meaningful. Prior to the session, post any pictures you have gathered around the classroom.

Warmup

Choose one of the following:

Servant Pictures

As students enter the room, point out the various pictures. Discuss the following questions. "What motivates people to do acts of service for others? Which service opportunities have you found meaningful? Why was the experience meaningful? How might Christians have a different motive for serving others?"

Or...

How May I Help You?

During the week before this session contact several adults. Ask them to volunteer 10 minutes of their time at the beginning of the class period. It might be especially meaningful to involve parents in this activity. Try to anticipate the number of students who will attend the session and have one adult for each participant.

The adults should be waiting as the students enter the room. For effect you could have the adults wearing aprons or carrying towels over their arms to identify them as servants. For the first five minutes in the session the adults are to do nothing but serve the students. They could serve them a snack, find them a comfortable place to sit, get a Bible for them, etc. They should convey the message by saying things such as, "Are you comfortable?" or "What else can I do for you?"

After five minutes call the group to order. Discuss the following questions with both youth and adults: "How did it feel to be served? How did it feel to be a servant? Obviously, the role of the servant was artificial in this situation. Can the role of a servant ever be forced? Why must any act of service be voluntary?"

You could invite the adults to remain for the rest of the class session. Their involvement in the commissioning service at the close of session might be meaningful. If you don't plan on using them again during the session, excuse them at this time.

Heart of a Servant

Distribute copies of "The Heart of a Servant" (Student Page 12). Ask for a volunteer to read the story aloud.

Many of the students will be familiar with Mother Teresa. Even if they have heard accounts of her life before, sharing her story again will set the stage for the balance of the lesson.

Following the reading say, "Having the heart of a servant, like Mother Teresa, means viewing things from a different perspective. It means seeing things through a servant's eyes rather than through the eyes of the world."

Be Transformed

Distribute copies of "Be Transformed" (Student Page 13). Participants will also need pencils or pens and Bibles. Allow the students to work independently, researching the Scripture references from **Romans 12.** In the blanks they should summarize the message presented. Monitor the students' work and assist them in discovering the proper responses. Typical answers might be as follows:

- **Romans 12:3**—Don't think too highly of yourself.
- **Romans 12:9a**—Be sincere in your love.
- **Romans 12:10b**—Put other people first.
- **Romans 12:16**—Don't be conceited.
- **Romans 12:17**—Do good things for all people.
- **Romans 12:19**—Don't seek revenge.

When the students have completed the assignment, call the class together. Divide the class into two groups. Ask the first person of one group to read the first statement under "Through the Eyes of the World." The first person in the other group should respond with the first statement under "Through the Eyes of God." The process should continue until all the statements have been read. For added effect you could instruct the students to stand on opposite sides of the classroom in single file facing each other. Ask that the first person whisper and that each successive person respond a little louder. The volume used should increase until the last person shouts his or her line in the loudest voice possible.

The message should be clear. There should be no need to discuss the activity any further.

Spiritual Gifts

Tell the students that servants come in all shapes and sizes. God has provided His church with a variety of gifts so that a variety of needs may be met.

Distribute copies of "Spiritual Gifts" (Student Page 14). Have the participants work independently. There are more than 25 different spiritual gifts mentioned in the Bible. Less than half of them are listed on the sheet. The ones listed are typical of those that young adults might possess, readily identify, and enjoy using.

Ask the students to read about the various gifts. After reviewing the gifts they are to circle at least two gifts, but not more than four, that they feel the Holy Spirit has given them. Allow five minutes for this activity.

When all have completed the activity, request that each participant find a partner. If there is an uneven number of participants, serve as a partner for one person. It may be helpful, especially if you are not participating as a student's partner, to model this activity by sharing the gifts you feel God has given you. Direct the students to share with each other the gifts they have circled and the reasons they believe that God has given those gifts to them.

My Mission Statement

Distribute copies of "My Mission Statement" (Student Page 15). Once again, the students are to work independently. In the space provided they are to list the spiritual gifts that they have identified. They are also to complete the sentence stating how they plan to use the gifts God has given them.

Allow five minutes for this activity. When you sense that all participants have completed the task, move on to closing worship.

Closing

Choose one of the following:

Free to Serve

One option for marking the completion of this study of Romans is a service of commitment. The emphasis on servanthood during this session provides an opportunity for the participants to commit themselves to lives of discipleship in Jesus' name through the power of the Holy Spirit. A brief service is an excellent way of ending the lesson and the unit.

Be aware that some participants may be visitors or students who have attended only this session. They may feel less prepared to participate in this service. Assure them that their participation in the closing is an affirmation of what God is doing in our lives through His Word. As we study God's Word and hear about others, like Mother Teresa, who reflect God's Spirit in their lives, God prepares our hearts for such service. Remind them that our focus is always on Jesus Christ, who became a servant for us by going to the cross to pay for our sins. Our response to such love can only be this: "How can I serve others in His name?"

Distribute copies of Student Page 16A and 16B and songbooks. Recruit volunteers to read the prayer of Invocation and the Scripture reading from **Matthew 28:18–20.** Have each participant identify a partner with whom they will feel comfortable sharing their words of commitment.

Possible traditional hymns include "Take My Life, O Lord, Renew" (*All God's People Sing* 223) or "Christ Be My Leader" (*AGPS* 81). Possible contemporary songs to use include "We Are the Church," and "We Are His Hands." You may substitute other hymns if you choose.

Or ...

Circle Prayer

Close with a circle prayer. The prayer will provide the students with the opportunity to express their thoughts. Remind them that their words do not have to be eloquent or lengthy.

Begin the prayer with the following petition: "Loving Father, You have given us the wonderful opportunity to hear the Good News of Your Son, Jesus. Today You have challenged us to consider what it means to be a servant in His name. May those words cause us to reflect on Your will for our lives ..."

Following the opening petition, allow time for individual participants to share their prayer thoughts. When all students who desire to pray have done so, conclude the prayer with the following thought: "May our prayers be granted according to Your good and gracious will. In Jesus' name we pray. Amen."

The Heart of a Servant

Agnes Gonxha Bojaxhiu was born in Skopje, Macedonia, on August 27, 1910. She was of Albanian descent, but her family had settled in the country of Macedonia, located just north of Greece. Her modest upbringing in southeastern Europe would in no way compare to the place where she would spend all of her adult life.

In 1928, at the age of 18, Agnes left home to travel to Ireland. She had decided to dedicate her life to serving others. She was going to be a Catholic nun.

Her training was cut short because of the pressing needs of people. Within six weeks Agnes was sent to Calcutta, India, to be a teacher. Her work exposed her to the pathetic living conditions in this impoverished Indian city. The more she saw the more she desired to help. She studied nursing. Eventually she moved from the nunnery into the slums, living in the midst of the people. In time she founded the Missionaries of Charity, a congregation of women dedicated to helping the poor. This Roman Catholic order helps the poor, the sick, the disabled, and the dying. As part of her ministry, the leper colony Shanti Nagar was built.

In Rome, Pope Paul VI had made note of Agnes' dedication to her work. In 1968 he summoned her to Rome to establish a home for the poor in that city. When her work in Rome was completed, Agnes returned to Calcutta, where the Missionaries of Charity had continued and expanded their work. In 1989, a heart attack forced her to resign her position as head of the order. In a short time, however, she was fitted with a pacemaker, voted out of retirement, and returned to her post. As recently as 1996, she continued to lead the Missionaries of Charity on a limited basis.

In 1979 the world recognized the work of this dedicated disciple of Jesus Christ. She received the Nobel Peace Prize, and the name by which Agnes was known as a nun became a household word—Mother Teresa.

Be Transformed

Through the Eyes of the World	Through the Eyes of God
I'm number 1!	Romans 12:3
Say what's needed to get you what you want.	Romans 12:9a
Use other people to get ahead and then forget them.	Romans 12:10b
I deserve everything that I've earned.	Romans 12:16
People get what they deserve.	Romans 12:17
Revenge is okay.	Romans 12:19

Do not conform any longer to the patterns of this world, but be transformed by the renewing of your mind.
(Romans 12:2a)

Romans, Student Page 13

Spiritual Gifts

PROCLAMATION	I have the ability to speak in front of a group. (Ephesians 4:11)
TEACHING	I have the ability to instruct others. (Romans 12:7b)
WISDOM	I am able to look at a situation and determine what needs to be done. (1 Corinthians 12:8)
KNOWLEDGE	I possess a lot of information that I can use to help others. (1 Corinthians 12:8)
SERVING	I enjoy doing things for other people. (Romans 12:7)
HELPING	I look for opportunities to help others. (1 Corinthians 12:9)
LEADERSHIP	I find that people are willing to trust me and follow my directions. (Romans 12:8)
ADMINISTRATION	I am able to organize things so that tasks get done. (1 Corinthians 12:28)
GIVING	I enjoy sharing what I have with others. (Romans 12:8)
MERCY	I am a compassionate person who is sensitive to the feelings and needs of others. (Romans 12:8)
ENCOURAGEMENT	I am able to offer support to others as they seek to carry out their work. (Romans 12:8a)
DISCERNMENT	I am able to look a situation and confidently know the right thing to do. (Philippians 1:10)

My Mission Statement

God in His grace has given me, a redeemed child of God, the gift of salvation through faith in Jesus Christ. By the power of the Holy Spirit, God has also given me specific gifts to use to benefit others. These spiritual gifts may include the gifts of

_____

_____

and

_____

_____.

As Jesus' disciple I am going to use these gifts to

_____

_____

_____

_____

_____

_____

_____

_____

_____.

Free to Serve

Opening Song

Use a song such as "A Time to Serve" (AGPS 53), or another song or hymn.

Invocation

Leader: In the name of God the Father, God the Son, and God the Holy Spirit.

Class: Amen.

Prayer

(Read by a class member): Loving Father, we are completing a study of Your Word of grace to the Christians in Rome in Paul's day—and to us. We have heard the Good News presented in a powerful way. We thank You for this experience and for providing us with a loving and caring teacher. Now move us to follow You as disciples. We pray this in the name of Jesus Christ, our Savior. Amen.

Commitment

Leader: Sisters and brothers in Christ, you have heard God's Good News of salvation.

Class: Yes, and we believe that Jesus Christ gave His life for us so that our sins are forgiven and we look forward to eternal life in heaven.

Leader: You know that being a disciple of Jesus Christ requires commitment.

Class: Yes, and we are willing to make that commitment to be loving servants in the name of Jesus, as God enables us through His Spirit.

(Have participants sit facing their partners. One person will speak the words of commitment. Then the other will say, "Go in God's peace." Then, that person will repeat the words of commitment, and the first person will respond with the words of peace.)

Leader: Listen to God's word from Matthew's gospel, chapter 28:18–20. "Then Jesus came to them and said, 'All authority in heaven and on earth has been given to Me.

Free to Serve–continued

Therefore go and make disciples of all nations, baptizing them in the name of the Father and of the Son and of the Holy Spirit, and teaching them to obey everything I have commanded you. And surely I am with you always, to the very end of the age.' "

Having heard Jesus' command, now express your desire to follow Him by speaking the printed vow to your partner.

Youth *(spoken individually to partner):* I, _____, know that Jesus Christ is my Lord and Savior. Strengthened by my faith, I am now ready to leave here today and walk as a disciple of Christ. I am confident that God, through the power of the Holy Spirit, will grant me a servant's heart. I also trust in Him to give me the power needed to be an effective disciple.

Response: Go in God's peace.

(After each person has had the opportunity to share these words, the leader will close with prayer.)

Leader: Lord, hear the prayers of these Your people. They humbly desire to serve You. May they, through the power of the Holy Spirit, be granted the power and strength to be effective witnesses. In the name of Jesus Christ we pray. Amen.

Benediction

Leader: Go in peace and serve the Lord.

Class: Amen.

Closing Song

Use a song such as "Brothers and Sisters in Christ" (AGPS 78), or another song or hymn.